Un-Common Sense

For Real Women in the Real World

Suzette Brawner
and
Jill Brawner Jones

New Wine Press

New Wine Ministries
PO Box 17
Chichester
West Sussex
United Kingdom
PO20 6YB

Scripture quotations are taken from the following version of the Bible:
NIV – The HOLY BIBLE, NEW INTERNATIONAL VERSION.
Copyright © 1973, 1978, 1984 by International Bible Society.
Used by permission of Hodder and Stoughton Limited.

ISBN 1-903725-58-5

Typeset by CRB Associates, Reepham, Norfolk
Cover design by CCD, www.ccdgroup.co.uk
Printed in the United States of America

Contents

Dedication

What Others Are Saying About Un-common Sense

"*Un-common Sense* is uncommonly good. From the heart, Suzette and Jill have given us a book filled with humor and encouragement while poignant and inspiring. Enjoy!"

June Hines Moore
Speaker, consultant and author

"I sat down to preview this book but ended up reading until I finished it! A winner in every sense, it's full of wit, wisdom, and life-changing concepts. Once you open it you'll see why I didn't want to put it down."

Debbie-Jo White
Vice-President, Kanakuk Kamps

"I felt like this book was written for me! Loaded with humor and wisdom, it's a must read for women of all ages. I wish, as a rite of passage, that *Un-common Sense* was required reading for all thirteen-year-old girls. They would be so well equipped to face the real world."

Kay Nielsen
Lemon grove owner

"*Un-common Sense* is a valuable reminder that there are no excuses, no easy answers, and only one chance to live life. What a treasure to have such wise and witty insights captured together in this book, providing some welcome encouragement along our journey through life."

Melissa G. Pardue
Washington DC policy analyst

"An important book for any woman looking to establish her identity in confusing times. A breath of fresh air filled with simple answers for complex questions. An empowering experience, a hearty meal for a hungry soul."

Terin Alba
Singer/songwriter

"*Un-common Sense* inspires the feminine heart to get back to the essentials in life."

Rachelle Trank
American sign language interpreter

"When common sense comes up short *Un-common Sense* is your go-to tool for ready-to-use advice. This mother-daughter team has compiled a practical and humorous handbook based on life experiences and biblical wisdom we can all apply in our lives."

Deborah Lapides
Pastor's wife

Acknowledgments

Without our family and friends cheering us on, this book would never have been written.

Thank you:

- ▶ Jim Brawner: Big Daddy; patriarch of the Brawner family, idea-giver, proofreader, prayer warrior, dream believer. There is no one like you.
- ▶ David Jones: Analytical thinker, contract screener, thought provoker, endless motivator. Your life is a testimony.
- ▶ Jason and Alison Brawner and Travis and Kari Brawner: Story makers, example givers, tireless listeners, energy providers. Your strength and commitment are motivation.
- ▶ Jackson Brawner and Jameson Brawner: For the comic relief and for reminding us what really is important!
- ▶ Fred Bollen: Dad, Paw Paw: For the daily dose of "You can do it!"
- ▶ Debbie and Mitch Raymer, Gregg and Gail Howard, Marian Ralph, Louis and Deborah Lapides: For reading, praying, believing and encouraging.

▶ Paul Ralph: For your guidance, vision, belief and perseverance.

▶ Tim Pettingale: For all of your work, patience and confidence in us and in the project.

Foreword

I have devoted the majority of my life to producing products that I hoped would enrich the lives of couples and singles in all of their relationships. I have had the privilege of meeting people from all walks of life across the world and I have found one thing to be true regardless of where I travel: everyone has a compelling desire for strong and meaningful relationships. It is in the essence of who we are as human beings.

When Suzette and Jill told me they were writing this book, I was delighted. I met the Brawners when six-month-old Jill was perched on Suzette's hip. And then just a few years ago I was honored to officiate Jill's wedding. Over time our two families have worked, played and traveled together, laughed, cried and weathered the storms. I have had the opportunity to watch them make the journey through every phase of life and there is one thing for sure. This is a family that has those strong, meaningful relationships that we all want.

This book is for anyone who is in search of a fun-loving, challenging life lived to the full! It will cause you to think and consider, smile and laugh and finally, say, "That's so true!" Suzette and Jill share elements of common sense that can get overlooked while we are out pursuing life. You will see yourself in their stories and illustrations, trying to find the balance God intends. You'll catch yourself looking forward to turning the page to see what's coming next. Their combination of sagely wisdom and fresh perspective will leave readers of every age encouraged and motivated. They are simply my favorite mother/daughter team. This is a read you will surely enjoy.

Dr. Gary Smalley
Author of *DNA of Relationships*

Introduction

"Common sense is the knack
of seeing things as they are,
and doing things
as they ought to be done."
(Harriet Beecher Stowe)

As we enter the twenty-first century we are offered more educational opportunities than anyone could ever have dreamed possible. Instruction begins in the crib because standards are constantly being pushed higher and higher. Groundbreaking research is at an all-time high. Computer technology is changing and improving at the speed of light. There is a class or a "how-to" book for everything we might want to learn or experience. Universities are having trouble building enough parking lots to accommodate their enrollments. More progress and advancements have taken place in the last fifty years than all of history. It is mind-boggling to think that the musical birthday card that is tossed in the trash today holds more computer power than even existed before 1948.

Progress is amazing and exciting. But even though we are surrounded by knowledge, when it comes to living we seem to know less and less. What used to be common sense is something that appears to be slowly fading into the background. There is no arguing that life today is extremely complex and we live at a break-neck speed trying to "get it all done". We run like rats through the maze of life trying to figure out our way. No wonder we are worn out.

We hope you will slow down long enough to relax, read this book and smile while rediscovering some things that might be filed away in the far reaches of your mind. Pushing aside all the complexities we are tangled in and breaking things down simply is so restoring.

If we could not only engage our minds but our hearts as well, we might find some of the balance and peace we are all desperately searching for. God didn't give us life as a formula to be solved, but a journey to be enjoyed. We hope your trip is an exciting one.

Suzette Brawner
and
Jill Brawner Jones

You Are the Boss of You

*"Privilege and responsibility
are two sides of the same coin."*
(Author unknown)

Justin walked into the opening day of first grade with Erika, his mother, on his heels. Dressed in his freshly ironed shirt and shorts and new top of the line, name-brand sneakers, his hair was combed so perfectly that it was tempting to pat him on the head and accidentally mess it up a little. Pushing past all the other children and their parents, Erika approached the twenty-year veteran teacher who was greeting everyone at the front of the classroom. "Hi,

Mrs. Simpson. This is Justin and he is very excited to be in your classroom this year. Justin is extremely smart and is an exceptional child," she said, straightening his shorts and wiping a spit-moistened thumb across his cheek.

"He deserves special attention because he is really sensitive. He needs to sit right at the front of the class," she smiled admiringly, babbling on as wide-eyed Justin stood by hanging on her every word.

As she pointed to Justin's assigned desk two rows back Mrs. Simpson grinned knowingly and said, "There is Justin's desk. You might want to help him get settled in. I will be by to see if you have any questions after I visit with all the other very special students who are waiting to get their desk assignments."

A bit shocked at the teacher's response, Erika shuffled her son to his desk grumbling about it not being a front row seat.

In fifth grade Justin's teacher explained during a teacher conference that he was falling behind. Erika's exasperated response was that it was the first grade teacher's fault because Justin didn't have a front row seat. In eighth grade at parent/teacher night the math instructor expressed concern with Justin's lack of motivation to finish his work and turn it in on time. "The problem began in fifth grade when Justin fell behind. You know his teacher just didn't give him enough individual attention," Erika rationalized.

In his sophomore year in high school the principal called Justin's parents in to let them know that he had cheated on a history test. Their response was that if the tests weren't so hard Justin wouldn't feel it was necessary to cheat. In his senior year, after he sent threatening mail to several students, Justin explained in the vice principal's office that it was because he didn't get the lead part in the school play and he was tired of being picked on. It was all the drama coach's fault.

He struggled through college and law school transferring in and out of classes trying to find professors and situations that would accommodate him. His marriage failed after three years because, "his wife's family never really accepted him." After moving from law firm to law firm he landed in jail for embezzling from his partners. "It was the firm's fault because they just didn't move me up the ladder fast enough," he explained. "What else was I to do?"

The saddest part is that Justin couldn't see the common denominator in all of his problems. It was not the first, fifth, eighth or tenth grade teachers. It wasn't the drama coach or his ex-wife's family; not the professors or the law partners. Justin's problem was Justin. When asked what he thought the thread running through his troubled life was, Justin just stared at the counselor as if he had been asked a trick question.

Dr. Albert Ellis, a renowned psychologist says, "The best years of your life are the ones in which you decide the problems are your own. You do not blame them on your mother, the ecology, or the president. You realize that you control your own destiny."

It is an interesting facet of our strange human nature. There is no shortage of those to take credit when things go well, but no one wants to take responsibility when things fail. We place blame then run away from accountability like someone who has just lit a gigantic firework display. We blame our spouses for our financial woes, our children for our marital disharmony, our parents for our buried anger, our jobs for not having enough time at home, the school for our children's poor performance, the church for not enough biblical teaching and guidance, McDonalds for our weight gain, and the government for everything else.

> **There is no shortage of those
> to take credit when things go well,
> but no one wants to take responsibility
> when things fail**

There is no question when it begins. "It's Jimmy's fault! No it's not! It's Tommy's fault!"

That shouting match is as familiar as the aroma of a gym class locker room. The unanswered question is, when does it stop? Mature is the person who refuses to make bogus excuses and maintains some sense of personal responsibility. The weakest excuse we use is: "That's just the way I am and I can't help it. It's my personality." As my Dad would say, "That's a bunch of malarkey." A person who constantly shirks responsibility and places blame everywhere except on himself does not have a personality handicap – he is an irresponsible person. Why do we continue to play this game long past the time we are assumed to reach maturity? The truth is, if we continue to dodge responsibility we sabotage success in every area of our lives. The most discouraging thought is that children are watching and we are hatching a new generation of blamers.

> **Mature is the person who refuses to make bogus excuses and maintains some sense of personal responsibility**

Remember when you used to say in frustration to your brother or sister, "You are not the boss of me!" Well, it's finally true. You are the boss of you. Maybe we each should take a personal inventory and begin to take our boss duties seriously. We are in charge of the choices we make about how we live and how we act.

There is no doubt that we live in a fast spinning world. We are all tugged in multiple directions with things to do, people to see, and places to go. It is amazing, though, that some are able to accomplish twice as much as others in the same twenty-four hours. It's almost as if those people get an extra couple of hours every day smuggled in from somewhere. I have found out their secret! They are the bosses of their schedules. They have made definite choices about what matters most in their life and have sifted out everything that is not important.

We find ourselves exasperated with our life schedule and blame it for our stress. The most freeing thing is to finally realize that we, for the most part, set our schedules by the choices we make. Granted you may work and raise a very busy family, but no one forces you to serve on two community boards and three church committees as well as preside over the ladies' golf association. Good news! You get to choose. You are the boss.

> **In the long run, even though it might be a hard thing to do, it is better to say no in the beginning than say yes and fail to live up to your commitment**

After we have made our choices, we need to be responsible in fulfilling the commitments we have made. We all know people who are hyper-involved, bouncing from one thing to the next not really taking care of anything. They want us to believe that they have everything under control, yet they are the first ones to pass the torch of blame when things don't go as planned. In the long run, even though it might be a hard thing to do, it is better to say no in the beginning than say yes and fail to live up to your commitment.

Again, we need to remember kids are watching. It's a fact they learn by what we do way more than what we say. What are we screaming to them when we fail to keep our word and then blame everything from traffic to the dog throwing up? They are seeing, "Hey, if things don't work out it is surely not my fault." Our goal should be to launch them into the world as reasonably sane, responsible adults. When they enter first grade it's a lot of work for them to keep their loaded backpack from flopping them to the ground like a turtle on its back. When they graduate from high school they need to have more than the ability to handle the book load. The most valuable thing they can walk away with is an understanding of how to handle responsibility. The best way for them to learn how to do that is to see adults meet life head-on and manage consequences good or bad. Otherwise the cycle continues and the blamer gene passes to the next generation.

Several years ago, I picked up coffee and sweet rolls for a friend whose mother was scheduled for surgery. I thought the treats and some conversation would serve as a distraction during the long wait. I walked into the hospital waiting room just in time to see several family members heading for the door. "What's going on?" I asked as they stormed toward me.

"Oh, Mom's surgery had to be cancelled because when they did the blood work, some sort of count was out of kilter because of a medication she is taking," one of the family members huffed. "I can't believe that doctor didn't catch it before now. I took two days off work and flew in just for this!"

"I guess you really can be grateful the doctor did catch it. That could have been serious in the operating room," I answered.

"I guess. Who is in charge of all this anyway?" he sighed.

I wanted to say so badly, "Your mother or whichever family member is helping her should be the one in charge." I kept my mouth shut knowing he really didn't want an answer. It was a reminder to me once again that we are in charge of ourselves. This woman was seeing four different specialists and failed to give a complete list of her medications to the doctor before surgery. It could have killed her. If you can't be the boss, then recruit an executive assistant to take over for you!

Do you realize that taking personal responsibility can reduce stress and eliminate a huge number of arguments? If someone verbally comes after you for something you did, you can instantly calm them down by assuming responsibility for your failure and apologizing. It takes two to argue and if you refuse to engage in a verbal war and own up to your mistakes, the person who is angry will either calm down or look really strange trying to argue by himself.

> **Do you realize that taking personal responsibility can reduce stress and eliminate a huge number of arguments?**

Kari waited until Travis had a day off to take Jameson in for one of his well-baby check-ups. Travis was a medical resident at the time and he looked forward to his sparse time off like a six-year-old anticipating Christmas morning. On the way to the office, Kari assured him that the in and out time should only be thirty minutes tops because this doctor ran such an efficient office. At that Travis relaxed. He really wanted to spend the morning with Kari and Jameson at the zoo, not cooped up in a doctor's office.

After they checked in at the reception desk Travis sat down on the floor with Jameson. As he dumped out the basket that was sitting in the corner he wondered how many little slobbery mouths and snotty noses had recently played with the toys. Thirty minutes later, when he had configured the blocks in every way he could think of, he looked at his watch, then Kari. "I am sure it will only be a few more minutes," she assured him. "This has never happened before."

Travis took a deep breath and picked up little books to read to Jameson while another thirty minutes passed. Finally he got up and said, "Something has to be wrong," as he made his way through the crowded waiting room toward the desk. After explaining that they had been waiting for an hour the receptionist excused herself saying she would be right back. When she returned she immediately ushered them to an examination room. Within three minutes the doctor came through the door. "I can't begin to tell you how very sorry I am that you have been waiting for so long," she began. "Your time is valuable and we have wasted it! When you checked in it was accidentally entered into the computer that you missed the appointment. I wasn't even aware that you were here. Please forgive me."

"Oh, that's OK," Kari said. "Computer errors happen," she continued almost feeling badly for the doctor.

"No, it's not OK. That should have never happened," said the embarrassed doctor.

Every bit of anger and frustration that Kari and Travis might have felt melted like sugar in hot coffee. The doctor could have blamed the computer, the receptionist, or even the busy schedule, but instead took full responsibility for the mistake. By doing so, it instantly calmed everyone down including the office staff. She was the boss and she was assuming her boss responsibilities.

An unusual amount of common sense is something called *wisdom*. It is intriguing to me that how deep wisdom runs doesn't always fall directly in proportion with the amount of education and the number of degrees someone may have. In the big picture those with commitment to responsibility and integrity come out on top.

Your life is just that; *your* life. *You* are the only one in charge of *your* emotions, *your* behavior and how *you* live. Just remember to do the best you can with what you have at the time and own up to the results; both the good and the not exactly what you had hoped for. One of my mentors and one of my favorite people on earth was Spike White. I had the amazing privilege of calling him friend for thirty years. Every once in a while he would grab my shoulder, give me a hug and say, "Suzette, always pray like it all depends on God and work like it all depends on you. Then give credit to God for His blessings and assume responsibility for your part."

> **The key to being an effective boss**
> **is to remember that with**
> **position and privilege comes**
> **a lot of responsibility**

So today, if you haven't already, declare yourself "the boss of you". The key to being an effective boss is to remember that with position and privilege comes a lot of responsibility. Congratulations and good luck on your promotion!

Something to think about...

▶ In what departments of your life do you need to take your boss duties more seriously?

If in Doubt, Don't

"The world would be better off if people paid as much attention to their consciences as they do to their neighbors' opinions."
(Author unknown)

The auditorium began to fill with college co-eds anxious to hear the savory wisdom of a woman old enough to be their mother. For some odd reason it is different listening to someone older and wiser when it isn't your mother. Maybe it is just easier to swallow the truth when it's served up by a stranger. As she approached the platform in her flawlessly pressed blue shirt, I was quick to notice that it only made her matching blue eyes brighter. While we were taking our seats, the girl beside me nudged me and said, "What a classy looking lady!"

I smiled in agreement and proceeded to get settled in. The speaker started her presentation with a story that forever changed my perspective on life. She opened with the simple statement, "If in doubt, don't." Then she began to explain.

> ## Maybe it is just easier to swallow the truth when it's served up by a stranger

The audience instantly connected with her as she took us back to when she was our age. At twenty she married her college sweetheart. A successful football player, he was just short of the NFL draft. However, a nasty injury late in his senior season ended that dream. To follow his passion, after graduation he took a job as the head football coach at a well-known high school in the south.

Their life was full and soon they started a family with the birth of a son and two years later another son arrived. Her husband was living a coach's dream: a quarterback and a receiver. Content with their family size they soon made plans for permanent birth control. After all, life was comfortable; no need to complicate things. So the urologist's appointment was set for a Friday afternoon.

Like many Monday mornings she took her sons to the neighborhood park to run off some of that boy energy.

This day was strangely different as an overwhelming wave of sadness washed over her. She described it like the rain cloud that occasionally follows Charlie Brown in a Peanuts cartoon. The boys were blurting out loud belly laughs as they chased each other around the playground equipment on this beautiful sun-drenched day. Other mothers were smiling as they pushed their kids on the swings. But she felt alone, as though she was stranded on an island with nothing but hurricane waves pounding the shore. Depression was not something she battled, but this sure felt like what others described. Trying to shake it, she rounded up the boys and took them to McDonalds. After ordering the comfort food of her choice she sat down and stared at it. Her appetite must have gone wandering with her mind.

She went home, put the boys down for a nap, and began to examine everything that could have brought on this unfamiliar feeling. While surveying a mental checklist, the realization of what was weighing her down hit her like a linebacker at full speed.

She wasn't really ready to stop watering her family tree, or was she? Two children were plenty ... maybe not? For a moment she thought she was just going through hormonal shock or some weird female thing, but then she recognized that she needed counsel and knew just where to find it.

Still sleepy from their naps, she gathered up the boys and drove to the high school and dropped them off at football practice with their dad. Taking a deep breath she drove down the familiar road where the family attended church.

Not much older than her, the pastor had been a personal friend for years. Explaining she only needed fifteen minutes of his time, the secretary ushered her into the office.

After listening to a short explanation of how she was feeling and why, the pastor leaned back in his chair and smiled. "You know, folks spend most of their lives making decisions the hard way when it is actually a simple process," he said.

"Really?" she asked looking a little puzzled, since this decision didn't seem to have a right or wrong answer.

"It all boils down to four words: *If in doubt, don't.* It's like we have a built-in decision maker and most of us never take advantage of it. It not only can help us make decisions, it can also help keep us out of trouble."

"Wow," she sighed. "I definitely have huge doubt, so I guess 'don't' is the answer."

"Maybe for right now," the pastor answered. "Timing in life is everything. You may feel totally different about the same issue in the future, but if right now you have doubts, I would say don't."

She thanked him and left the office feeling like the rain cloud that had been following her had just evaporated. She met her family back at home and explained to her husband the emotional ride she had been on. He was a bit surprised at the cancellation of the doctor's appointment, but totally agreed with her rationale.

The auditorium was strangely quiet as everyone con-sidered what the speaker had just shared. Then she surprised us all by adding with a catch in her voice, "I am forever grateful for the wise counsel from my friend and pastor. You see, two years after that meeting I gave birth to my daughter, Jill, who is here today."

I sat flabbergasted as several turned in my direction and smiled. Needless to say, I am really glad Mom learned this simple concept when she did. I wouldn't be here if she hadn't listened to the tugging on her heart. What is so amazing to me is that she had no doubts, after having me, that her family was complete. I just probably confirmed that more than three children would have left very few of her brain cells intact.

We all have a built-in decision maker as I found out that day. Since then, I have chosen to make decisions based on the simple theory, if in doubt, don't. The trick is listening to your heart. God's Holy Spirit gives us direct prompts and it is our job to be still long enough to hear them. He doesn't shout. We run our lives at such a frenetic pace that many times we make decisions and just chalk up that uneasy feeling to bad gas from the Mexican combo platter we had for dinner. It helps if we slow down long enough to breathe and consider all aspects of our decisions. I have learned to run them through a grid of sorts before coming to a final conclusion. This doesn't pertain to minor daily decisions, like where to have lunch, but the major ones.

First: I have learned to not make important decisions quickly. Pray, asking for wisdom and discernment. I came by that revelation the hard way. Consider all of the pros and cons by drawing a line down the center of a piece of paper and writing them down. This is amazingly helpful. Wait a little while before making the final decision. Often you wake up the next morning and everything looks different than it did the night before.

> ## Consider all of the pros and cons by drawing a line down the center of a piece of paper and writing them down

Second: Seek wise counsel. It is helpful to get the opinions of those you trust and respect. I have found that it is not smart to ask for more than a couple of reliable advisors. After that, it becomes a committee and you know what that means. Will Rogers once said, "Outside of traffic, there is nothing that has held this country back as much as committees." Know, however, that the final decision is ultimately yours and you must live with the benefits or consequences.

> ## "Outside of traffic, there is nothing that has held this country back as much as committees."

Third: Timing is everything. If something is not a good decision now, it does not necessarily mean that it won't be a good decision later. This, of course, depends on what you are considering. Some things are just always going to be a bad decision! Remember, if in doubt, don't can keep us out of trouble too.

Fourth: Learn to differentiate between an honest doubt and being scared of change. If we hesitate at everything that we question, we go nowhere. Finding the balance is the key and that is a continual search.

I wish I could say that if you ran every decision you need to make through this simple process, *voilà*, there you have it – a perfect answer! Obviously, life is not that simple. Besides, if it were, it would be so boring. I have found however, that if I slow down long enough to pray and listen to my heart, seek wise counsel, and not make hasty choices, it helps take the edge off the stress in the decision making process. I also know that there is a time and season for everything in life and what may be a wrong decision today may be a right decision in the future. Probably the most complicated thing for me is figuring out what is true doubt and just plain being scared of change. Figuring that out, I know, will take a lifetime.

> ## Learn to differentiate
> ## between an honest doubt
> ## and being scared of change

Reflecting on that day in the auditorium with two hundred other girls, I had no idea the valuable lesson I was about to learn. It truly changed my life. However, if you think about it, the concept is so simple: if in doubt, don't. I guess that is when my journey began gathering valuable information: some uncommon sense.

Something to think about...

▶ Can you remember a time when you were in doubt but went ahead as if the doubt wasn't there?

That Is No Way to Win Friends and Influence People

"He who guards his mouth and his tongue
*   keeps himself from calamity."*
(Proverbs 21:23)

Since I haven't played lately, I don't know if the rules have changed in the game of Jacks. When I was a kid everyone agreed, before we got started, that each player was allowed a certain number of "Do-Overs". A Do-Over was good to use at any time during the game when you missed. It was a chance to rewind and start over as if the goof-up was never made. If it was an extremely competitive day we would all agree that no Do-Overs were allowed, but if we had the whole afternoon for a long, leisurely game, several were given. I loved Do-Overs because that meant there was some grace for mistakes.

Karen, Phyllis and Ruthie were regular players and sometimes Melinda and Cindy would join us. My front porch was the arena of preference. Because it faced north, it was the coolest place to be on a hot, summer afternoon and the concrete slab made the ball bounce to perfection. Our Jacks games were famous and one time even a visiting granddaughter of the neighbor on the next street over came to play. She was from another part of the country and obviously wasn't aware of the Jacks rules and regulations of Arkansas. She questioned everything we did and amazingly she had never heard of Do-Overs! At one point about fifteen minutes into the game after Phyllis had patiently explained one more time what a Do-Over was, our visitor had apparently had enough. She jumped to her feet, got right up in Phyllis' face and screamed so hard her face turned red, "You are a fat slob stupidhead and you don't know the first thing about playing Jacks." Then she picked up the jacks and ball and threw them as hard as she could out into the grass and stormed down the driveway. Stunned, we all looked at Phyllis who had started to cry. Very calmly Karen said to Phyllis, "Too bad she doesn't have a Do-Over for that!"

One deep philosophical observation from my ten-year-old friend broke the tension and made us laugh until we were all lying on the cool pavement. I was so grateful for Karen and what she said not only for Phyllis' sake, but also for mine. It is something I have always remembered.

Oh, if life were so simple and we all had Do-Overs for what we say. You may not have called anyone a fat slob stupidhead lately (or maybe you have), but do you ever wish that the words that come out of your mouth could be edited? Many times I shock myself and think, "Did I just say that out-loud or is it still rolling around in my head?" Much of the time my mouth functions about ten times faster than my brain. I can get myself into real trouble. Surely there is a disease name for this condition?

Our mouths are so powerful. We can encourage, praise, show love and appreciation, or we can discourage, degrade, ridicule and even destroy with what we say and when we say it. So often we are extremely careless not only about *when* and *what* we say, but also *where* we say it. It amazes me to watch parents talk about their three-year-old while she is standing right next to them. Most little kids are not hard of hearing they are just short. Why do we talk about them as if they are in another building?

> **We can encourage, praise,
> show love and appreciation
> or we can discourage, degrade,
> ridicule and even destroy with
> what we say and when we say it**

It is also a good idea not to discuss sensitive issues or information that you don't want passed on with those short people in your presence. It's not a matter of *whether* it will be repeated, but *when*. Without a doubt it will be at the most inopportune and embarrassing time. Ask any kindergarten teacher. They have heard enough stories to write a steamy script for an award winning soap opera.

On our very first family vacation my parents came into the full understanding that kids assume whatever adults say must be fair game to repeat. Mom, Dad, my brother, Russ, and I were staying at a resort on the beach in southern Alabama. It was one of those places people would go and stay for a week. The same faces greeted us every morning in the dining room and throughout the day around the property. While we were there so was an older woman who had long, stringy, dyed black hair, wore bright red lipstick outside of the lines, always had a scowl on her face and never smiled. She was almost scary, especially to two little kids. Every time we saw her my parents made some remark to each other. One morning, toward the end of our week, as we were leaving the very crowded dining room, Russ, who was four at the time, stopped at her table. The lady looked at him with that familiar scowl. He very innocently and like it was a good thing said, "I thought you would like to know that my parents think you look just like a witch."

He was so polite it was as if he were extending a huge compliment to her. Something amazing happened. She smiled. Mom and Dad just kept on walking. Kids are so honest and just haven't reached the age of knowing how to be tactful.

Apparently age doesn't always determine when one learns about tactfulness. We smile when children innocently say things that shouldn't be shared. We even excuse teenagers for a lot of things that come out of their mouths because their brains are very confused by random hormonal attacks. But what about when we become adults? We all know those who could be the poster people for this unnamed condition. When we run into them at the market or the mall we try to mentally forecast what outlandish thing they will say or ask. To add to it, their voice volume is usually set on high. Do you ever find yourself looking around to see who could be overhearing the conversation?

Grocery stores and shopping malls aren't the only places conversations are overheard. Theaters, restaurants and sporting events put you in hearing distance of things that you might find interesting and then some stuff that makes you want to put your fingers in your ears and hum real loud. At the first game of the football season in my son Travis' senior year in college, I found myself by one of these people who had a mouth with an editing handicap. Travis had a really successful junior year and was named first team All-American. When someone is at the top of anything people generally tend to pick them apart and find fault. It must be some recessive gene of meanness found in humans. I ended up sitting directly in front of one of these guys when Southwest Missouri State faced the University of Tulsa. The 100-degree late August heat in a jam-packed stadium in Oklahoma was enough to set anyone on edge, but this man just about pushed me beyond. As the kicker and punter Travis was continually running on and off the field. Every time he would step onto the turf the critic had something negative to say: "Yeah, sure this guy is All-American. Who voted for that? Are you kidding me? You call that talent? Where did this kid come from? Geez, I could do better than that!"

Apparently age doesn't always determine when one learns about tactfulness

---

I tried the fingers-in-the-ears-humming-technique during the first quarter with very little success. About half way through the second quarter when he yelled, after Travis kicked a field goal, "Good grief, how did this guy ever make it out of high school?" something came over me I still can't quite explain. I jumped up out of my seat, turned around and grabbed the bottom of his shorts and screamed in some primal tone, "Hey! Do you have a son on that field?"

He was shocked and I was probably more shocked. "No," he answered, shaking his head back and forth like a seven-year-old boy who had just been caught hitting a girl.

"Well, I do!" I snarled back at him through gritted teeth. "And every time he sets foot on the field you make some smart, critical remark and I am tired of listening to it. I don't want to hear it any more!"

Quickly nodding his head, he said, "OK," and slowly sat down.

I almost felt sorry for the guy. Almost. He really didn't bargain for the menopausal mother of the kicker to be sitting in front of him. Who knew? How do any of us know who is hearing what we are saying? We should all learn from his mistake.

Sometimes we actually say something to someone on purpose in the heat of the moment and have no idea how what we are saying is going to affect us later. I saw a church marquee not long ago that said, *Don't Burn the Bridge Today That You May Need to Walk on Tomorrow*. That concept needs to stay in the top drawer of our memory file because it can help keep us out of tall weeds most of the time. The sales clerk you are so rude to today may just be the CEO of a company you need a favor from ten years from now. The person you cut in line in front of at Burger King this morning may be the highway patrolman that stops you on the interstate this afternoon. A casting director who was auditioning a young actor early in his career didn't know who she was talking to when she told him, "You have no talent, you are no good and you might as well give it up." She was surprised years later when he approached her while she was casting for one of his famous movies to say, "I remember you."

> ## Don't burn the bridge today
> ## that you may need to walk on tomorrow

"You do?" she replied quite flattered, hoping the people close by heard him since he was such a megastar.

"Yeah, you are the one who told me several years ago that I had no talent, I was no good and that I might as well give it up. I didn't like your negative attitude then and I don't now. You can leave my movie set."

She hadn't burned the bridge; she had taken a stick of dynamite to it! I really think our mouth should come with a warning label! It can be as dangerous as one of those bottles of poison with a skull and crossbones. Yet, the best warning we can heed is written plainly in Proverbs: *"He who guards his mouth and his tongue keeps himself from calamity."*

The fascinating thing is that less than ten percent of what we communicate is expressed with our words. The rest happens with body language, facial expressions and tone of voice. Remember when your mom would say, "Don't roll your eyes at me when I am talking to you!"

> **The fascinating thing is that less than ten percent of what we communicate is expressed with our words**

Without a word, rolling eyes say, "I can't believe you are making such a big deal out of this. Good grief, you just don't understand. Give me a break!" Who on earth teaches kids, especially girls, to roll their eyes? We grow up into women with a natural talent for communicating very loudly without saying a word. Because I am so verbal, generally when I am quiet, Jim instantly picks up that

1. Dale Carnegie, *How To Win Friends And Influence People*, Pocket, re-issue edition 1990.

something is off. Even sometimes when I just want to be quiet, he thinks something is wrong. So what we don't say usually says more than what we do say.

That is probably why the written word can be so misunderstood. With so much of life being lived through e-mail I have figured out that I need to be even more careful about what I say and how I say it to avoid offending others. Sometimes we can get away with confronting someone face-to-face with a smile and they will walk away not knowing what just happened. However, when we hit the send button, so much more can be misinterpreted because of the absence of body language, tone of voice and facial expressions. I found myself back-peddling real fast once because of a trail of misunderstood e-mail communication. That is one situation in which I failed to win a friend for sure. I don't think real resolution ever happened, but I did the best I could. Once again, I learned something the hard way, but at least I learned something. Be careful what you send electronically. Remember, it is not like an intimate conversation. It can be copied word for word and forwarded on to others.

My daughter-in-law, Alison, is a family and children's counselor. She sees some pretty heartbreaking circumstances on a weekly basis. Some of the saddest situations are dealing with angry people who spew horrible, hurtful things out of their mouths and through e-mail and wonder why their relationships are in a shambles. When explaining the damage that words can do she sometimes hands a new tube of toothpaste to the client and asks him to squeeze all the contents out of the tube onto the table. After enjoying the task, generally he sits in curious expectation of what she is going to do next. Then she calmly asks that every last drop of the paste be put back into the tube. "That's impossible," he usually complains.

"Yes, it is," she answers. "That is how it is with your hurtful, mean words. Once they are out they can never be taken back. You can say you're sorry, but the wounding words are still out there never to be gathered-up. Be careful how you use your words."

If you want to gather honey, don't kick over the bee hive!

One of my parents' favorite authors was Dale Carnegie who in 1936 wrote the book, *How to Win Friends and Influence People.*[1] It was quoted from frequently in our house when I was growing up. The title of the first chapter is, "If You Want to Gather Honey, Don't Kick Over the Bee Hive!" Many times in my life I have realized, after it was too late, that had I kicked over the beehive and had to painfully suffer the sting of what I had done. I guess when it comes down to it, if you want to get anywhere in life, you basically have to be nice to people. For some that is easier than others. Like everything else, you have a choice to make about how you treat people and then you live with the results of that choice.

Mom was all about choices and she especially loved Dale Carnegie. When someone was rude or would do something dumb she would look at me and say, "That is certainly no way to win friends and influence people." She had a choice in the way she handled thoughtless people. After becoming an adult, though, I realized that Mr. Carnegie actually helped Mom keep from saying what she really wanted to. What she really wanted to say was something like, "That person is a fat slob stupidhead," but then again, that is certainly no way to win friends and influence people.

Something to think about...

▶ Do you control your mouth or does it control you?

Laugh and the World Laughs with You ... Cry and Your Make-up Runs

"Humor is to life what shock absorbers are to the automobile."
(Author unknown)

Mom used to say to me, "Suzette, life is about choices and you really only have two when it comes to happiness. You can laugh and the world laughs with you or you can cry and your make-up runs." Laughing at life instead of worrying and taking everything so seriously is as natural as breathing for some, but for others it is equal to asking them to walk a mile on their hands. It just doesn't seem to be possible.

I, by nature, am a very task oriented, black and white, linear thinker. Life is simple that way – not too much gray, ebb and flow; everything is cut and dried . . . close to dull. Jill, by nature, could not be more opposite. Life is an adventure, change is exciting, and every day for her is like a child arriving at a playground full of shiny new toys. I remember that feeling the first day of school when I opened the door for recess in second grade. I can even smell the fresh sawdust and remember the configuration of the jungle gym. Somewhere along the way I got lost in the growing up process, forgot that feeling and have to make a conscious effort every day to remember how refreshing it is. Jill and I are so different it is a miracle we even like each other. She must have been blessed with her father's not so serious gene.

I like everything in order, organized without surprises. A mentor friend pulled me aside several years ago and said, "Suzette, you like all of your ducks in a row and Honey, they just don't come that way."

Through time I have discovered that *my* ducks usually fly in every direction, even though I covet them to be in precise formation like the Canada geese over Lake Taneycomo. Jim has even accused me of taking two weeks to be spontaneous. I'm not that bad, but close. I literally have to be the watchdog of my emotions and my need for everything to be under control. Time has mellowed me some, but it is still a daily awareness.

I guess I look at a problem like a possum in the road. You just hit it and keep on going

---

Jim, on the other hand, skips through life with the attitude that every day is a privilege. Once at a small group lunch everyone was asked to share what stressed him or her most. One by one we named our top two or three stressors. When it was Jim's turn he paused for a minute and said, "I really can't think of anything. I guess I look at a problem like a possum in the road. You just hit it and keep on going. Now, if you hit a dog or a cat you would stop, but a possum ... you keep on going. It is not worth the trouble to stop."

That was a true revelation for me, almost spiritual. I am trying to look at problems like possums now. Hit them and keep on going.

I was privileged to have a wonderful peek into my daughter's heart on parent's night when Jill was in the fourth grade. Earlier in the semester the teacher had asked the kids to write a paper about the key person in their life. It was in a key shaped, brightly colored folder. I should have had a clue to what her life was going to be like. She colored outside of the lines then and still does. I was certain when I sat down at the little desk to read her work that it would be about me. After all, I was her mother! To my surprise the opening words read, "The key person in my life is my Daddy." As I read on, I understood. Her paper continued, "He teaches me to snow ski and to water ski." And with her nine-year-old wisdom she summed it up: "But most important, he teaches me not to take life so serious." At nine she had it figured out! Why did it take me half of my life to realize how important that simple concept is? And the process continues.

There have been numerous studies done on the amazing benefits of humor and laughter. A good belly laugh not only can break up a tense moment, it acts as a safety valve that actually shuts off the flow of stress hormones. These stress hormones can in reality suppress the immune system and raise blood pressure. They also activate the fight or flight response when we face stress, anger or hostility.

> **A good belly laugh not only can break up a tense moment, it acts as a safety valve that actually shuts off the flow of stress hormones**

After I learned about the destructive forces of stress and the benefits of laughter, I implemented an imaginary friend. You are never too old for an imaginary friend, you know! My friend is a little man dressed up in a security guard's uniform who dashes over to shut off the flow of the stress hormones, closing the safety valve with all his might every time I begin to laugh. I try to imagine this each time I am faced with a potentially stressful situation. Just that vision makes me smile. Have you ever laughed so hard that you have been rendered helpless and can't move? I have and I bet you have too. We need that in large doses and often. I think we take too lightly the Proverb that so clearly explains, *"A cheerful heart is good medicine."* Humor and laughter are so good for us. Now if only the facts could travel from our brains to our hearts.

> ## "A cheerful heart is good medicine"
> ## (Proverbs 17:22)

Humor has an amazing diffusing power over fear and anger. It is similar to that *stop, drop, and roll* drill you learned when the fire marshal paid a visit to you in elementary school. Fear and anger seem to push a button that causes us to run around, mostly in circles, thinking something will be resolved or that we might just feel better. All the while we are adding fuel to the fire. Humor is like the roll part of the drill. It can totally squash the fire.

The first time I became keenly aware of this was one sweltering summer day when I had my three kids and a friend's son at the swimming pool. The kids were leaping off an apparatus that bounced the jumper into the pool. Six-year-old Jill didn't weigh enough to sail through the air into the water, so she climbed up and just jumped on the edge, which was probably only an eighteen inch drop. Everyone was enjoying so much fun until Jill hit her elbow on the metal frame breaking the large bone in her upper right arm. I was more traumatized than she was. I kicked off my shoes as I ran to the edge of the pool to make a dramatic water rescue that I had learned fifteen years earlier. She came to the surface and began swimming toward the side of the pool with one arm before I ever hit the water. Then she very frankly stated to me that gymnastics would probably be out of the question for the next couple of months. Thinking that her favorite swimsuit might have to be cut off her was her greatest concern. I was consumed with the fact that there was probably not a doctor alive that could put her arm back together since at this point it looked as if she had an extra elbow halfway up her arm.

By the time we got to the hospital I could feel that grip of panic closing around my throat. It was Memorial Day weekend and the emergency room looked similar to the mall on the Friday after Thanksgiving. After we finally found a parking space and got inside I was barking out orders to the medical staff like a drill sergeant on a mission. Jim was nowhere to be reached. He always told the boys that whenever he was unavailable that they were in charge. Twelve-year-old Jason took this very seriously and sensed that at any moment I might tear into an x-ray technician or nurse like a momma-bear protecting her cub from serious danger. He sauntered over to me and tapped me on the shoulder just as yet another person was about to become my verbal abuse victim. "Mom, could I talk to you for a minute? " he asked. At first I ignored him but he persisted.

"Mom, I really need to ask you something."

"What?!" I wheeled around. Jason at twelve was already a head taller than I was and has a smile that would comfort anyone, but the look on his face was very serious.

"Does this mean that we can't play golf today?" he solemnly asked.

"Jason!" I answered in a shrill.

"Mom, I am only kidding, but geez you are going to have to lighten up or you are going to explode or injure someone."

Jason obviously got the not-so-serious gene from his dad too, and at that moment I was extremely grateful as I began to smile. The little man in the security guard uniform had just rushed over to the stress hormone shut off valve.

> ## The little man in the security guard uniform had just rushed over to the stress hormone shut off valve

Is there a person in your life that you watch and he or she is not even aware of it? It is a bit scary to think that someone might actually be watching you in turn. I guarantee there is. The person I like to watch is Michael at Wal-Mart. He makes me smile because he always smiles. I have watched customers chew him out because something is out of stock and he responds with a grin saying, "Oh, it should be in by Tuesday." He is always laughing and teasing with the customers as he stocks the shelves and bats down complaints like flies on a hot day. I want to be more like Michael. One day when I was trying to figure out why he smiles and laughs so much I came to the conclusion that he had to be on serious medication or that he owned original Wal-Mart stock. No one is that happy without reason. Or are they? Then I realized that he too, probably had an imaginary friend in a security guard uniform that handles the valves in his life. However, Michael's imaginary friend has to have a bunch of buddies backing him up. Maybe I need a security guard crew instead of just one friend.

> ## "I believe that life is 10% of what happens to us and 90% how we react to it"
> ### (Chuck Swindoll)

Life is stressful. There is no getting around it. Chuck Swindoll once said, "I believe that life is 10% of what happens to us and 90% how we react to it." So it looks like there are really only two choices: take life too seriously and cry, or laugh and hit the possums in the road and keep on going. Mom was right once again.

Something to think about...

▶ In what area in your life do you need to "lighten up" a little?

If You Want to Be Treated Like a Lady, Act Like One

*"I think that somehow
we learn who we really are
and then live with that decision."*
(Eleanor Roosevelt)

I grew up with two older brothers, a dad, and with Cooper as my best friend. I swam on the swim team, played softball, basketball, volleyball and ran the anchor leg of the 4 by 100 meter relay that still holds the high school record.

I could do more chin-ups and outrun plenty of the guys. I pumped gas and changed tires like a member of a racecar pit crew. Friends from my childhood will tell you I was a tomboy with a capital T. At the same time I was all-girl and totally obsessed with pink.

Starting out my life surrounded by males was a huge advantage for me. They challenged me, protected me and didn't let me get away with whining. None of them ever fell for the, "I am a girl so I can't do that" line. When I was in high school someone said to my brother Jason, "Man, I feel sorry for any guy who tries to mess with your sister because of her two big brothers."

Jason shot back, "I feel sorry for any guy who messes with Jill, not because of me or Travis, but because of Jill!"

I learned a lot about being a girl from my brothers because clearly they helped me create a much-needed balance.

Society can't seem to decide what is "right" for women

Society can't seem to decide what is "right" for women. We have traveled through the years of being absolutely helpless, totally dependent weaklings, to hard, independent "I can do it all and all by myself" super women. With the rules constantly changing, how are we ever to know what being a lady looks like, let alone how one is supposed to act or how one should expect to be treated? Fortunately the pendulum seems to be swinging back to somewhere in the middle. You can be a strong, independent, stand on your own two feet type of a woman and at the same time be a lady. I think the secret is for the scale to strike a healthy balance.

> **You can be a strong, independent, stand on your own two feet type of a woman and at the same time be a lady**

The first thing we have to figure out is who we are. Some of us may feel like that is equivalent to being on a cross-country road trip without a map. Shakespeare wrote, "Know thy self and to thine own self be true." How can we be true if we don't know who "thine own self" is?

I was recently in an entertainment class with a brilliant teacher who challenged us to discover the core of who we are. As I scanned the room the night of our first class, I realized that I was looking at a fruit cocktail of people. They ran from a homely looking science geek to a racial activist, to a Vanna White type. I thought, "How in the world can we all be here to learn the same thing?"

The teacher explained that most of us would spend our lives trying to fit into a box or category. Her lesson to us was to find who we are and live it out to the fullest. If you choose to be a teacher, teach the class that everyone can't wait to get to. If you want to be a doctor, study the latest diseases and make new discoveries in areas that no one else has attempted. If you are an artist, don't reproduce

Van Gogh, but create a masterpiece then proudly sign your name.

> ## ...most of us would spend our lives
> ## trying to fit into a box or category

Her point was: run your own race and run it hard. I ran track in high school and one day when I got to school I realized that my running shoes had stayed at home. Coach Pock was never one for excuses, so I thought I'd better find some shoes or I would be running the hill the next day. The first person I asked was my very responsible friend, Jonya, and of course she had an extra pair "just in case". We wore the same size shoes so it worked out perfectly ... kind of. The shoes were so well broken in and molded to her feet that by the end of practice my feet were blistered and bloody. I could barely walk. Coach questioned why my form was off and why my times were slower than usual. I was trying to run my race in somebody else's shoes.

> ## ...run your own race
> ## and run it hard

In the same way, many women blister their hearts attempting to fit into places they don't belong, simply because they don't know who they are. The challenge is to find out who you are, what your talents are and what you want to experience during the short time you are given here on earth, then pursue that life. I was in a restaurant not long ago and there were ten "Paris Hilton wannabe" girls waiting to be seated. It struck me like lightning that our generation, like many others, truly suffers from identity theft! We don't know who we are and it is too much trouble to figure it out, so we just try to become a knock-off of someone else. How sad!

In the movie *Runaway Bride*, Julia Roberts' character was fighting to find her identity. She had been engaged four times, but each time literally left her groom standing at the altar as fear caused her to turn and run out of the church. Consequently, she had become the brunt of everyone's joke in town. A reporter, working on a front-page story about the famous runaway bride, discovered something interesting about her. He curiously asked each former fiancé what kind of eggs she liked. One by one they told the reporter how they liked their eggs cooked and added, "She likes them the same way I do."

She didn't even know how she enjoyed eggs. She was adjusting her likes and dislikes to the fiancé of the moment. It wasn't until the reporter pointed out to her that she wavered on most decisions, that she realized she didn't know what she wanted for herself. She was merely latching on to what other people wanted for her. Him saying to her, "You are so lost that you don't know how you like your eggs," caused her to take a strong look at her life and how she was living it.

So many of us do just that. We follow what everyone around us thinks we should like or do or have a passion for when it couldn't be further from reality. We need to know ourselves, find a direction and press forward. Have you ever really stopped to think about what you want out of life? I would challenge you to take an inventory of your dreams, hopes and desires, then concentrate on how to make them happen. If you don't have a plan you will spend a great deal of your life flying around like a bottle rocket without a stick: going all over the place with no direction, eventually exploding or fizzling out. Don't let others steal your dreams with their expectations. Find out who you are!

> **If you don't have a plan
> you will spend a great deal of
> your life flying around like
> a bottle rocket without a stick:
> going all over the place with
> no direction, eventually exploding
> or fizzling out**

Truly knowing yourself produces confidence. It is not cockiness or over assurance, but knowing who you are and being comfortable with who you are that produce a gentle confidence. A popular actress being interviewed after receiving a coveted Hollywood award was asked, "You have played the same role for several years and now all of a sudden the awards are rolling in. Why do you think that is happening?"

Her response is something that has stuck with me.

She answered, "Well, you know I think that simply I am finally comfortable in my own skin and I guess people see that."

I realized that despite all the changes in hair and clothing styles over the years, she was the same person. She eventually understood who she was, relaxed, and that gentle confidence spilled over into her work and the awards followed. Her best work started after she became content with who she was.

That isn't only true for TV stars. We can do our best work, live our best life, and love the deepest when we come to the point where we are content with who we are. We all know people who just seem to be happy with themselves. They are such a pleasure to be around. They are easy to talk to and work with. They tend to make you feel "comfortable in your own skin". It actually has nothing to do with their size, shape, or color. Gentle confidence is an inner quality that is an overflow of knowing who you are.

These past few years I have come to realize that I was truly blessed living in a family that really encouraged me and nudged me to step out and do things that built confidence. I know not everyone has that. If you didn't or don't, I would challenge you to start today realizing that you are special. You are totally unique. God created you like no one else on this earth and you have a purpose that no one else can fulfill. My acting coach, Bob Luke, said to me once, "Jill, it is sometimes best to get at the back of the high dive and run and jump without looking back." Often I wonder if I am brave or just crazy enough to step out and not look back. For me that is what it took to build some confidence. And it is a continual process.

We will never be respected if we cower and constantly apologize

Sometimes the missing puzzle piece in developing gentle confidence is connected to discovering that if we expect respect, we get it. We will never be respected if we cower and constantly apologize. If you meet someone who gives you a limp handshake, won't look you in the eye, and continually ducks her head, you know that she doesn't expect respect. And guess what? She is guaranteed not to receive it. Nine times out of ten that woman came from a background of demeaning talk with no encouragement. She started life without a support system. Scripture reminds us, *"God did not give us a spirit of timidity, but a spirit of power, of love and of self-discipline"* (2 Timothy 1:7). We have a God-given essence that should expect respect. We are valuable even though we don't feel like we are. For some, understanding that we are worth something and deserve respect comes down to making a basic decision like choosing where to have dinner. It is just a conscious choice of placing the facts over feelings.

"God did not give us a spirit of timidity, but a spirit of power, of love and of self-discipline."

On the other hand, many of us have the misconception that if we demand respect we will be held in the highest esteem. Wrong! We may seem to be honored to our faces, but are called Jerk and worse behind our backs. Nothing holds truer than what you learned in kindergarten: Do unto others as you would have them do unto you. Don't expect respect from others if you have a reputation for stepping on whoever is in your way to get to where you want to go. Whatever you throw out there will come back to either honor you or kick you in the rear end. Respect is something we *earn*, not demand.

Somewhere in the middle is the ever-fleeting balance. To complicate things more, not everyone agrees on what being respectful is. Growing up in the South, "yes ma'm" and "yes sir" were expected. Some of my northern friends think that it is sassy and rude for children to address adults in that manner. One friend refuses to have the door held open for her. She has her reasons and I respect her choices. Every woman sets her own standards.

I, in contrast, wait for the door to be held open for me. I see it as having the red carpet pulled out for five seconds. I gently asked one of my first high school dates that the five-second carpet be rolled out. He pulled up at the house and honked as though to say, "Come out, I'm ready to go." Dad wasn't thrilled about the whole dating thing to begin with and this just confirmed what he had already decided about most high school boys – they're like bird dog pups. They know they have fleas, but they just don't know where to scratch. I had a split-second choice to make. For me, a lady is to be honored, respected and for heaven's sake met at the door. So I very patiently sat in the living room listening to him honk. It only took about a minute for him to realize that if we were going out, he would have to come in. When we got outside he settled into the driver's seat and started the engine, leaving me standing at the passenger's door smiling at him through the window. He rolled down the window and asked why I was standing outside the car. I simply said, "I thought you might have wanted to open the door for me and just forgot."

He shot out of the car and dashed around to open the door. As you can probably guess, that relationship didn't make it too far. Years later I ran into him and he actually thanked me for that uncomfortable episode. I by no means think it is our responsibility to train men. I do, however, adamantly believe it is our job to stand firm and know we are worthy of being honored in the manner we choose.

When it all comes down to it, if we truly want to be treated like a lady, we have to act like one. How old we are, where we came from, and what we look like has nothing to do with how we should be treated. Finding out who we are, developing that gentle, not overbearing, self-confidence that is our God-promised right, and expecting respect, definitely do. The twenty-first century offers us more opportunities and choices than ever before. Our life is similar to a lavish buffet at an over-the-top party where we get to pick and choose what we want to do and how we want to live. Being treated like a lady along the way just makes the trip more interesting.

Something to think about...

▶ If you could write the script for how you want to be treated, how would it read?

Who Ever Told You Life Was Going to Be Easy?

"Character cannot be developed in ease and quiet. Only through the experience of trial and suffering can the soul be strengthened, ambition inspired, and success achieved."
(Helen Keller)

Even though Labor Day had come and gone and summer was officially over, Peggy and Burt wanted to squeeze in one more outing on the boat before it had to be put away for winter storage. They packed a picnic lunch and headed to the middle of the calm, smooth-as-glass lake for an afternoon of much-needed "nothing but relaxing". The normally busy lake was seeing fewer and fewer boats as October was quickly approaching. Finding a quiet place to stop and drift was not the usual challenge. After an hour or so of enjoying submarine sandwiches and idle conversation, Burt decided to take a break from the hot, late September sun and jumped in for a swim. Since the nights were now cooling off considerably, the water temperature was perfect. After a few minutes he yelled to Peggy who was cleaning up the lunch leftovers in the boat. "Burt?" she answered, surprised to see panic on her husband's face. "You OK?"

"If you don't get over here fast you are going to have a drowning husband!" he answered, trying to remain calm.

She quickly got the boat started and in gear as it had drifted about thirty feet. By the time she reached him, he was powerless and starting to sink. She instantly turned off the engine and jumped in. Grabbing him and holding his face above water, she began yelling as loudly as she could for help. Peggy knew there would be no way she could get this big guy back into the boat by herself. She was just over five feet tall and Burt, at six foot three, outweighed her by at least a hundred pounds. Amazingly, she treaded water for an hour praying that someone would hear her shouts. Finally a fisherman noticed the commotion. He got to them just in time to rescue Peggy who was about to give in to exhaustion, but it was too late for Burt. In that hour Peggy lost her husband. My husband, David, lost his father.

I can't even imagine what they must have gone through. David, fourteen, was now without a father and Peggy, in an instant, became a single mother. Life had taken a shocking and unexpected turn. Peggy and Burt had just started a new business. She was now left to take care of their clients, raise a son who was reeling from his father's tragic death, and somehow find her own strength just to survive.

Desperate to find the identity he had lost, David searched every dead end imaginable hoping to fit in somewhere. He wound up with a rough crowd and was out on his own at seventeen. Just as Peggy was starting to regain the balance that had been knocked totally off kilter from her husband's sudden death, she now faced the challenges of a rebellious son.

Life doesn't follow a script and there are no guarantees

In his senior year of high school David finally realized he was tired of running from himself and worn out from being so angry over the loss of his dad. A friend and mentor, Joe White, helped him redirect his life back on track. Joe reminded him that his earthly father may be gone, but his heavenly Father would always be there to guide, direct, and comfort him. Besides, there were so many people who loved him and wanted the best for him. The change in David was nothing short of incredible. Because of the trials he encountered and pushed through, he has had the opportunity to give hope to hundreds of kids who have faced overwhelming obstacles. He has been able to encourage in a way only someone who has been down that painful path can. Peggy has also been an inspiration to others who didn't think they could make it through the toughest times imaginable.

Life doesn't follow a script and there are no guarantees. No one ever told us it was going to be easy. Many times life lets us down because what we have planned is the polar opposite of what actually happens. I remember over-hearing a conversation after Travis' high school football team lost in the first round of playoffs after posting an undefeated regular season. Eric was a couple of years older and had come back from college for the game. He slapped Travis on the back and said, "You know Trav, sometimes life just bucks up and kicks you in the rear and this is one of those times. But I guarantee that the sun will come up in the morning."

The one choice we do have is how we handle ourselves when life hands us the unexpected

I was only in junior high, but I somehow understood what he meant. Life can get rough and be disappointing. We just don't get a choice about a lot of things. The one choice we do have is how we handle ourselves when life hands us the unexpected.

I heard a story about a farmer and his donkey. The donkey fell into an abandoned well and the farmer could not figure out how to get the donkey out so he called on several of his friends to help him. After much discussion, it was decided that the donkey was old and probably wasn't going to live much longer anyway. Each of the farmer's friends took a shovel and started filling up the well with dirt. The donkey cried and cried, but the men kept shoveling. The farmer noticed that the donkey was suddenly quiet. He walked to the edge of the well, looked in and was amazed at what he saw. Each time a shovel-full of dirt hit the old donkey, he would shake it off and step on top of it; shake it off and step on top of it ... He continued until the dirt pile was high enough for him to climb out of the well.

We all are hit with shovels full of dirt every day. Some days it seems like a dump truck backs up and unloads. Just like the donkey though, we have a choice: either shake it off and step on top of it or let it bury us. We decide.

We all are hit with shovels full of dirt every day

With everything that hit Peggy and David, they made the choice to shake it off and step on top of it. Sadly many of us step in some mud and then complain about how much work it is to clean off our shoes. For the most part we are whiners. Instead of being grateful for the free gifts given to the first fifty shoppers at the grand opening of a new store, we complain because we wanted a blue one instead of the green one we got. What a waste of energy!

For many the biggest tragedy we will face today will be when we walk all the way to the back of the Super Center and the "Restrooms Closed for Cleaning" sign is up. That is an inconvenience not a crisis, but we react like our rights have been violated in the worst kind of way.

The key is if we *react* or *respond*. It is so easy to have a knee-jerk reaction and let our emotions take over. Again, we have a choice. We can either chew out the innocent maintenance man who is only doing his job or go find another bathroom. Another choice is, if it is truly close to an emergency, have someone guard the door and use the men's restroom!

We have to be careful about whining and complaining. Once we get started it is like our mouth is falling down stairs. It gains momentum and goes even faster with each step. I am the first to admit that we need to vent sometimes. I call my friend and warn her, "I just need to gripe. Do you have a minute?"

She just listens and says things like, "Wow! Oh, that's really bad! I am *so* sorry."

> **We have to be careful about whining and complaining. Once we get started it is like our mouth is falling down stairs**

After a few minutes I feel so much better and we drop it. She has the freedom to do the same thing with me. I learned the hard way once that you don't whine to a man.

Men see a problem and instantly go into "fix it" mode. That's great when you need a problem solved, but many times we just need a listening ear and sympathetic heart because the only thing that can be fixed is our attitude.

> ## Men see a problem and instantly go into "fix it" mode

We all have people in our lives that are a constant reminder that we really have nothing to complain about. Abi does that for me. I've known her my whole life and when we are together what we do, mostly, is laugh. She loves life and makes the Energizer Bunny look run down. After college she began a career that she had dreamed of: teaching and coaching. Then things took an unexpected turn and at twenty-six she was diagnosed with a rare life-threatening disease. She has been in the hospital so much that one hospital employee thought she was on staff. After enduring eighteen surgeries she had to leave her school position. She was heartbroken. Even though she takes numerous life-sustaining medications, her heart rate some-times drops so fast that she passes out. She has some sour lemons to work with, but she still manages to make her own brand of lemonade. Abi is the most popular patient at the hospital because of her concern and love for others. She talks to everyone making them smile and laugh. She has chosen to not merely endure life, but enjoy it to the best of her ability.

Recently I had the opportunity to sit down over coffee and dessert with this incredibly strong, determined woman. I asked her how she was doing. She said, "Jill, I am really doing fine. I do know one thing for sure. Life is too short and too precious. I don't want to take it too seriously and I don't want to have any more five cent conversations."

So that night we got to remember the past, laugh about the present, and hope for the future. Most of all we were real with one another. Instead of giving up she has a "bring it on" attitude. Sure it might be easier to just sit in the corner and not step out, because that way nothing bad will happen. But nothing good will happen either. Abi will never understand how much of an inspiration she is, not only to me, but everyone she meets.

> **Most of the time it is just simpler to look through the negative lens because searching for something positive in so many circumstances is too much work**

I hope you have an Abi in your life to remind you that how we see a situation is all about our attitude. We can look at it from either a positive or negative perspective. Most of the time it is just simpler to look through the negative lens because searching for something positive in so many circumstances is too much work. It is easier to look on the bright side when we see a light at the end of the tunnel and know for certain that it is not an oncoming train. Hanging on to our faith when things look so dark is often extremely hard. I know in the deepest part of my heart that my husband would not be the person he is today if he hadn't traveled down the winding road he did. Our life experiences mold us into who we are. We can use them to step on top of to get out of a hole, or we can let them bury us.

"The harder I work, the luckier I get."

My friend Jamie grew up living in the government projects. Today he runs several very successful businesses. I love it when he says, in his thick New York accent, "The harder I work, the luckier I get." No one ever told the little boy from Far Rockaway, Queens, who fought to get home from school every day, that life was going to be easy. He made a decision to take what life handed him and use it to his advantage.

Mom reminds me that life doesn't owe me anything. Life alone is a divine gift from God and we are left to decide what to do with it. Things that happen along the way write the story of who we are.

Life alone is a divine gift from God and we are left to decide what to do with it

Maybe we read too many make believe stories when we are young. Where do we get the idea that life is going to be some fairly-tale existence? Besides, that would be so boring and predictable. Truly life, for the most part, is not an emergency even though we often live it that way. It is when we realize it's a gift and a blessing, no matter what we may face, that the minor inconveniences and irritations that get shoveled onto us become just what they are – minor. Shake it off and step on top of them.

Something to think about...

▶ Do you use life's trials or do they use you?

If My Aunt Had Different Body Parts, She Would Be My Uncle

"The past is a guidepost,
not a hitching post."
(L. Thomas Holdcroft)

When I was a freshman in college, the United States was going though amazing cultural transitions. It was an era of rebellion and of pushing the limits on everything to the very edge. The Vietnam war was in full swing, civil disobedience was expected if you were an educated, progressive person, and peace marches or someone streaking naked though campus happened every day. Girls were burning their bras and "If It Feels Good Do It" and "Make Love Not War" was how most students felt. However, the Jesus movement was gaining momentum and most likely held enough balance to keep everything from totally crumbling.

I was one of those kids who didn't venture too far out of the box. I remember feeling totally civilly disobedient once when I ditched Biology class to hand out "Jesus Loves You" cards to angry war protesters. I found out quickly that the Jesus cards only made them angrier. However, one guy did stop shouting long enough to say he didn't want the card, but he sure liked my skirt. It was my favorite one and shorter than anything I would ever have let Jill wear out of the house. I am sure it was the prayers of my parents in addition to the enforced university curfews that kept me from making more not-so-good choices than I did that year.

There is a huge difference between hearing and listening

I remember hearing all of the warnings about the pitfalls to avoid during my freshman year from sophomore friends. I heard them, but didn't really listen. There is a huge difference between hearing and listening. However, I am one of those hardheaded people who learn the best lessons from their mistakes.

I guess I thought if I just carried those heavy textbooks around that I would absorb the necessary information, kind of like osmosis only not on a cellular level. So most nights after curfew, when I should have been studying, I was two doors down in Susan and Vicki's room having ordered-in pizza, M & Ms and soda, listening to the Beatles with a dozen or so girls in tie-dyed Peace T-shirts. The room was so smoke filled that it was hard to see let alone breathe. Even though I didn't smoke, it is amazing I escaped without some sort of permanent lung damage. We would tell stories, laugh and eat halfway though the night. I remember once saying, "College would be perfect if we just didn't have to worry about classes. They really kind of get in the way!" Then someone so rudely reminded me that that was why we were in college. Oh, yeah, that's right.

The big problem for me was that I had class every morning at 7:30am and I was running on about four hours of sleep every night. I was a college student and wasn't smart enough to figure out at the end of the semester why my grades stunk, why I had had three upper respiratory infections and why I had put on, not fifteen, but twenty-five pounds. That year I gained volumes of knowledge, though most of it was not from textbooks.

I thought I should let Mom know before I went home for Christmas that my grades were probably not going to be what she might be expecting and that I was a bit super-sized. It was extremely tempting to make up some wild story that I was marrying a guy I had met the weekend before, we were dropping out of school to join the Peace

Corps and that we would be shipped over seas in two weeks for a three year commitment. That way my mistakes wouldn't seem bad after I let her believe the bizarre story for a few minutes. It was a thought.

I finally called her and explained what a dumb mistake I had made wasting my first semester at college and that I was sorry. If only I had not been so stupid. She simply said, "Suzette, what's done is done. Saying 'if only' won't change anything. If is such a big word. You can say it all day long and things that have already happened still won't change. Think about it. Saying, *if* my aunt had different body parts she would be my uncle, doesn't make her your uncle. That is how far out there it is to not realize that the past is a closed chapter. Leave it alone and go forward."

"But it was such a dumb mistake," I whined.

"No, it was a mistake. Now, if you do the same thing again, that is when it becomes a real dumb mistake."

Sometimes, even now, when I think about that semester, I cringe. It wasn't until I sent my own kids off to college that I fully understood the sacrifices my parents made. Knowing that I had taken for granted what they had done for me burned like spilled hot McDonalds coffee. The positive out of it is that I did learn something.

If, as the Merriam-Webster dictionary defines it, means "in the event that". It really is used to suggest the circumstances that would have to exist in order for an event to happen. You can use if looking backwards or forwards. Obviously, like Mom said, the past is just that: past, over, finished. The only thing we can do is to learn from those past mistakes and make the necessary changes so history doesn't repeat itself. It doesn't do any good beating ourselves up, staying trapped in yesterday and continuing to say "if only".

> **The only thing we can do
> is to learn from those past mistakes
> and make the necessary changes
> so history doesn't repeat itself**

Once I heard a pastor say, "Stop wallowing in the past and get over it. That was yesterday and today is today. Yesterday ended at midnight." And even John Wayne agreed. He once said, "Tomorrow is the most important thing in life. Comes to us at midnight very clean. It's perfect when it arrives and puts itself in our hands. It hopes we've learned something from yesterday."

The pastor and John have it right. Pretty powerful and very clear. There are so many things we all wish we could go back and change. It's just a waste of mental energy! I have a friend who was in college the same time I was. She attended a major university on the coast and the activity outside the classrooms there made my southern campus look like a boarding school run by nuns. She is a loving wife, mother and professional woman. I ran into her adult son not long ago who I hadn't seen in years. I shared with him how much I admired his mom and what a wonderful woman she was. "I just love her. She is just so peaceful and down-to-earth," I gushed.

He looked at me and grinned, "It must be from all the drugs in the '60s."

"Oh, come on!" I answered.

"Well, it's true."

After I thought about it for a while, I realized that she was one of those brilliant people who learned from her mistakes, left yesterday alone and pushed forward. She knows it's OK to look back, but it's rude to stare. Our life is a culmination of our experiences, the good and the not so good.

Forgive yourself and go on. Forgiveness is hard sometimes, but what is exceptionally hard is forgiving yourself. You might be thinking: if only I had had a better childhood, if only I hadn't married such a jerk, if only I hadn't been through two divorces, if only I had run around with more responsible people. If only ... Forgiveness only happens when you finally give up the hope that the past could ever be any different and move on. The second half of Philippians 3:13 says, *"But the one thing I do: Forgetting what is behind and straining toward what is ahead."* So much is out there waiting and so many of us stay chained to the past like a dog leashed to a park bench trying to drag it around.

> **Forgiveness is hard sometimes, but what is exceptionally hard is forgiving yourself**

Not only do we find it hard to let go of our mistakes and stop saying "if only", we tend to think that *if* how we look and what we have were different we might be happier. We get so caught up in the web of comparison. The more we look at everyone else the more tangled we get. Then we wear ourselves out struggling to escape the web like a trout in a fish net. How destructive! If only I had a BMW or a Mercedes. If only I had a bigger house. If only I had the kind of job she has. If only I were taller I wouldn't be so fat. Do we think all that determines our happiness?

> **We get so caught up in the web of comparison. The more we look at everyone else the more tangled we get**

Everyone has at least one friend who always looks fabulous, has a loving husband, a clean home and obedient children. She juggles those responsibilities while she takes graduate classes, plays in a tennis league and a Bunko group and is in a couple of in-depth Bible study groups. To top it off she is a size 4. Every time I am with friends like that I secretly want to say, "Are you kidding me? You disgust me almost as much as Bobby Webb did when he turned around and sneezed all over my desk in second grade! You can't be for real."

But I just smile and listen to all of her latest endeavors and accomplishments. Those kinds of people set the bar so high that the rest of us wear ourselves out trying to jump over it. Stop it! We need to come to a place of acceptance and contentment with who we are and what we have. Each of us is gifted in so many different ways. As long as we continue to fall into the trap of "if only" we waste our time not enjoying our life and last I heard we only get one go at it. Besides, underneath it all, Miss Perfect Life is most likely a stressed-out mess.

> **Those kinds of people
> set the bar so high that
> the rest of us wear ourselves out
> trying to jump over it**

But *if* need not be a four letter word if it is used constructively. The best way to do that is to look forward instead of backward. "If I study I will make better grades and if I don't eat eight thousand calories a day I won't gain twenty-five more pounds" were a couple of things I had to consider after that first semester at the university. Possibility thinking is taking the "what ifs", using them to set some goals and considering a strategy to follow them through. The bite of the consequences from not so stellar choices may be enough motivation to push you into possibility thinking. It sure was for me. Positive action most of the time equals positive results. It takes a conscious effort to look at the positive "what ifs" instead of the negative "if onlys". Many times I find that to be extremely challenging. It almost swims totally against the way I think, but experts say that bad habits can be broken in twenty-one days. I think the place we need to land is somewhere in the complex balance between idealism and realism.

**It takes a conscious effort
to look at the positive "what ifs"
instead of the negative "if onlys"**

Clearly we shouldn't waste our time looking backward or around us thinking of the negative "if onlys", rather than looking forward and upward to consider all the positive "what ifs". And it's true that if my aunt did have different body parts, she would be my uncle. I just don't think that is going to happen. And that is as comforting as the smell of her cold cream.

Something to think about . . .

▶ Have you felt the freedom of giving up the past?

Always Look as Prosperous as Possible

"Like a gold ring in a pig's snout
  is a beautiful woman who shows no discretion."
(Proverbs 11:22)

After graduation, with some help from her coach, Michelle landed her first job with a major marketing firm. Moving on from college and her position as captain of the basketball team to a job in the business world was going to be an enormous change. But she felt good about closing one chapter of her life and stepping right into the next one. Her official first day was the Tuesday after Labor Day, however she had received an invitation to an end-of-summer picnic. She was surprised and quite honored that she had been included especially since it was at the home of the president of the firm. What an opportunity it would be to meet some of her new colleagues in a relaxed environment! Slowly reading the invitation she recognized the address as one of the more exclusive neighborhoods in town. That made the event all the more exciting and at the same time somewhat intimidating. She did relax a little when she saw the word "CASUAL" at the bottom of the card.

On the evening of the party she arrived right on time in shorts and her favorite flip-flops. Since she hadn't yet been at the office on a daily basis, she really didn't know anyone to call to see what others might be wearing. But how hard could it be? Casual meant casual. Right?

She found a parking place on the street and made her way up the long, curving driveway to the front of the exquisite home. After ringing the doorbell that gonged like royalty being introduced, she was greeted by the president's wife who was in a sundress and strappy little sandals. Instantly Michelle realized that casual back home and casual for this company meant two entirely different things. All she could think about was once hearing the phrase: "You don't get a second chance to make a first impression." It would be way too obvious to turn and run so she stuck out her hand, put on the best smile she had and introduced herself hoping that Mrs. president in the cute dress hadn't thought she was a delivery person. She had a fast choice to make. She could be miserable and feel stupid for making such an easily avoided mistake or make the best of the circumstances and enjoy the party. What Michelle had going for her was a magnetic personality and a truckload of confidence and she left for home at the end of the evening with a new group of friends knowing she did the best she could have done with the situation. She also made a note to herself to never assume anything. Always ask questions about unspoken expectations.

> ## "You don't get a second chance to make a first impression."

Like it or not, we live in a world of unspoken expectations. As frustrating as it may be, we are judged on appearances. It is an unwritten law of the universe. What makes it even more aggravating is the amazing airbrushed images of flawless women smiling at us from the magazine covers in the racks at the grocery store checkout. Those are the pictures that make us second guess letting the Rocky Road kiss the red scanner light, land in the bag, and head home for a good time on our hips. We are asked to live up to unrealistic expectations that even Barbie would have a hard time doing. You may feel like you were handed the leftovers when looks were being assigned. But I promise you that every woman, when asked, can instantly name several things about her appearance she would classify somewhere between slightly irregular and horribly wrong. Why do we all want what we don't have? Cheryl Tiegs, a gorgeous, highly successful model, once said, "Like anyone else, there are days when I feel beautiful and days I don't. When I don't, I do something about it."

> ## We are asked to live up to
> ## unrealistic expectations that even
> ## Barbie would have a hard time doing

I think the key lies in the "doing something about it". Evidently my great-grandfather was big on "doing something about it". He raised five girls on modest means and we credit him with saying, "There are no ugly women, only lazy ones. You should always try to look as prosperous as possible." I guess that was his way of insisting that you do the best you can with what you have. It basically comes down to this: *It's not what you have. It's what you do with what you have.*

We are born with a set of genes gifted from our parents. It is kind of like Christmas, but most gifts that we really don't like can be exchanged or returned. Our "genes gift" comes with a no refund/no return policy. I think it would have been nice if we had been allowed to go fishing in the gene pool for what we wanted. The truth is we don't always get what we want, we get what we get. We can't even blame our parents for the combination we end up with. There are so many different ways that traits can line up that only God could have orchestrated it. That's what makes each of us so unique, because no one on earth has the same genetic makeup as you do. Nobody can improve a Rembrandt original. It can only be restored, preserved and maintained. Where we get off base is trying to adhere to the world's standard of how we should look instead of taking care of what we have.

It's not what you have.
It's what you do with what you have

In high school so many of my friends struggled with their body image. Everybody knows someone who has fought with an eating disorder or may even have gone to battle with one herself. Why do we listen to the snide remarks, go on a diet with a best friend, and then let it become an obsession? What's really sad is that this mind game doesn't stop at high school graduation. What we look like seems to forever be in one part of our mind if not mostly in the front. Our image has a huge effect on how we feel about ourselves. This is why it is vital that we take care of our bodies in a healthy balanced way without becoming totally obsessed.

What we look like seems to
forever be in one part of our mind
if not mostly in the front

We may not be able to choose our DNA, but we can choose what we do with it. I've decided that women essentially fall into three categories when it comes to personal maintenance. If you just sit on a bench at the mall for about fifteen minutes you will instantly see what I mean. Coming from the left is the girl in really tight, low slung jeans wearing too much flamingo pink lipstick and so much hairspray that she may possibly lift off with an unexpected gust of wind. She has one of those little yappy dogs peering out of the top of her jeweled bag. Headed in from the right is a girl who is loaded down with packages with her hair barely pulled back in a ponytail holder wearing gym clothes that are ten years past their expiration date. The first is in the "trying too hard" category; the second in the "didn't even try". Every once in a while you will see someone in the third category: "makes it look easy". She is like the gymnast who effortlessly nails a back flip on the four-inch balance beam. This girl may not be head-turning gorgeous, but she definitely has it together and carries herself with confidence because of it. She has done the best she can with what she has.

The other day I was shopping and noticed another phenomenon that seems to be increasingly popular: mothers tying to look like their teenage daughters. I really don't know how to classify these ladies. Maybe in the "searching for lost youth" category? It's almost like a reversal of playing "dress up" in mother's clothes. The scary thing is that these women go out in public. I guess for me there is something just a little disturbing about the combination of ripped jeans and bifocals. I thought about it for a while then I called Mom. "Hey, I just wanted to thank you for always striving for class and for not dressing like a fifteen-year-old," I said.

A little puzzled she answered, "Oookay, thank you, Jill – I guess?"

I explained to her about the bifocal-ripped-jeans-cult and then asked her if she ever wished that she were younger. "Oh, I don't know. Sure it would be nice to have fewer wrinkles and all body parts a little further north of where they are now, but there would be a huge trade off. And nothing, not even a tight rear end, is worth going back to Algebra for. Besides, no matter how young or old you are there are going to be younger, prettier and more toned women. Right?" she answered.

Now that is profound uncommon sense.

> ## It takes the focus off the makeup bag and instills a sense of self-worth that Maybelline can never offer

Probably some of the best advice my grandmother gave my mom when I was born was, "Compliment her looks, but talk about her inner beauty ten times as much as her appearance." You know what I think this does? It takes the focus off the makeup bag and instills a sense of self-worth that Maybelline can never offer. What if we all put the "ten times as much" rule into effect? Conversations would sound something like this: "Wow, love those shoes! They go perfect with your grateful attitude. Those earrings really add to your listening ear and your kind words make that shade of lipstick look awesome!" If you actually said something like that to a friend she might suggest you take

the rest of the day off. I would challenge you though, to
experiment for a while looking past the outer shell of those
around you and focus on their positive character qualities.
Compliment them on their kindness and generosity as well
as their hot new jeans. They will become more beautiful to
you, I promise.

What character qualities are you painting in your life?

When we consider that who we really are is not only our
body but, more importantly, our mind and soul, it brings a
whole different color chart into play. God gave us a clean
canvas to work with. He handed us the brush and lets us
choose our own shades. What character qualities are you
painting in your life?

One of the earliest memories I have of Mom correcting
me was when my mouth would run ahead of me. She
would say, "Sister, that attitude is so unattractive." Even
though I was just a little girl, I understood the meaning of
an ugly attitude. Have you ever met someone you think is
so attractive until she opens her mouth?

Once I was in line behind a woman at a coffee shop
who had just placed an order for her daughter and herself.
After I ordered and grabbed my coffee I headed for the bar
that held the five different sweeteners and four choices of
milk and cream. The woman in front of me was at the bar
with a canister turned upside down pouring sugar into
one of the coffees. As I stood there watching her, she very

matter-of-factly turned to me and said, "I know it's a lot of sugar, but my daughter needs all the sweetness she can get!"

I knew one thing for sure. She needed more than sugar in her coffee and it might take a long time for her to revamp her ugly attitude. Meanness doesn't happen overnight and neither does sweetness.

Wouldn't it be great if we could take a shot of sugar, like liquid love, in the morning and be sweet for the rest of the day? Our shot of sugar comes when we make a decision about our attitude. Though we don't get a choice about our genes, we do get a choice about our attitude. It shows up on our faces whether we have makeup on or not. In fact, the best foundation you can apply is a quick assessment of your heart. I have a friend who makes an attitude decision every morning. She is such a pleasure to be with. When she leaves a room it is as if she leaves a wonderful fragrance and it is not her expensive perfume.

If you asked fifty people to describe "beauty" you would get fifty different answers. Beauty is truly in the eye of the beholder. The beauty that you look at, that is. More important is the beauty that isn't just skin deep. It's the beauty of a grateful and loving heart.

> **If you asked fifty people
> to describe beauty
> you would get fifty different answers**

Not long ago I saw an interview with motivational speaker, John Maxwell. He was asked if he thought a person could truly have a contagious spirit. He explained that our thoughts transfer to our actions and our actions affect those around us. I understand this to mean that not only does my "sugar shot" in the morning affect me, it has the potential to affect everyone I'm around during the day. Our attitude not only determines how our day goes, it has the potential to influence everyone we come in contact with.

You really can't judge a book by the cover. However, if the cover is intriguing a reader is more likely to want to see what is inside. The same is true with us. If we do the best we can with what we have, people are going to be motivated to get to know us. Too bad if we don't like it, appearance *does* matter. We have to remember that a balance of inner beauty and outer beauty should be the goal. It doesn't matter how much time I work on my exterior. If I am a mean, thoughtless, selfish person my day has been a total waste of my makeup. And we all know that makeup is way too expensive to waste.

Something to think about...

▶ Where is your focus? What steps are you taking to develop your "inner" beauty?

Who Died and Crowned You Queen of Judgment?

*"If you judge people
you have no time to love them."*
(Mother Teresa)

Late one evening, after a long day in the city, a business-man boarded the subway to return to his hotel room. Looking forward to a hot shower and room service for dinner he sat down in a car that was almost empty. The only other passengers on board were a man and his three young children. Trying to clear his head after a frantic day of negotiations, phone calls and e-mail he noticed that the children were getting louder and more out of control with each passing minute. The father was absolutely oblivious and seemed not to really care.

"Humph! Some father he must be," the businessman thought to himself. "These kids are not only about to step on my last nerve, but one of them is going to get hurt if they don't stop swinging on the poles and jumping off the seats. I would never allow my kids to behave like that!"

He tried to block out the noise and mentally go elsewhere as the subway carried him closer to that shower and dinner. Suddenly, two of the rowdy kids crashed to the floor wrestling and yelling in tones that would cause a dog to howl. He was amazed to see no reaction from the father who still sat motionless.

Finally, the businessman shouted over the noise, "Sir! Don't you think you should get your kids under control? Someone is going to get hurt if they don't calm down!"

Startled, the man shook his head to come out of the stupor he was lost in. "I am so sorry," he sighed. "Please forgive me. I hope they haven't bothered you too much."

"Right!" the tired businessman thought.

"You see," the father continued, "we just left the hospital and my wife, their mother, well, she just died and I suppose none of us really knows how to act or what to do. I really can't imagine what we are going to do without her."

It was as if all the air left the subway car as the businessman caught his breath, totally ashamed of his judgment of that father. "I am so sorry," he offered as he promised himself from that night forward to not make rash assumptions.[1]

> ## Why do we waltz through life thinking we have the right to judge and condemn?

I wish I could say that I have never done anything as thoughtless as what that man did, but I can't. And if you are honest, you are in the boat with me. Why do we waltz through life thinking we have the right to judge and condemn? The majority of the time we have about two percent of the facts and we draw drastic conclusions based on what little we know. Then we are bold enough to share with someone else our half-baked observations and the vicious gossip begins.

We all know people who seem to thrive on making others the topic of their discussions. Some of the stories that float around make your head spin. But who can filter out the truth from the juicy tidbits that are stirred into the conversation? Those who choose friends as the topic of the day make me a bit nervous. I figure if they will talk about others to me, that they will talk about me to others. Besides, who am I to make assumptions and judgments?

Bonnie was the church gossip and self-appointed monitor of the church's morals. She always stuck her nose into other people's business. No one appreciated what she did, however, everyone was a little afraid of her so no one had the guts to confront her.

**Those who choose friends as the
topic of the day make me a bit nervous.
I figure if they will talk about others to me,
that they will talk about me to others**

She made a big mistake though, when she accused George, a new member, of being an alcoholic, after she saw his old pickup parked in front of the town's only bar one afternoon. Bonnie told George and several others that everyone seeing his truck at the bar would know what he was doing. George stared at her for a minute and turned and walked away without denying, explaining, or defending himself. Later that night George quietly parked his pickup in front of Bonnie's house and left it there all night long.

Perhaps after becoming the target of her own poison darts, Bonnie thought twice about making assumptions before she informed the community of all the "wrong doings" of others. Her first mistake was not knowing that George was a carpenter and had been hired by the owner of the bar to do some remodeling. More importantly, she underestimated who she was dealing with when she picked on George. Besides, what business of hers was it?

To reduce the risk of reigning as "Queen of Judgment" there are three things you might think about when you hear or see things that frustrate or shock you. These reminders sometimes help keep my perspective in check.

First, assume the best not the worst. The day before my mother's funeral I decided to make a picture collage on foam board to display in the lobby of the church for the funeral. I felt like it might be a bright spot in all the sadness for her four younger sisters. I set out to find a Hobby Lobby craft store that I had seen in the neighborhood. I drove around the same three blocks in a sea of traffic for what seemed like forever looking for the Hobby Lobby. I was tired and grieving and I was very hungry. Finally, I saw a Barnes and Noble bookstore. I knew that they didn't have foam board, but they did have a Starbucks coffee shop and a cup of coffee and a muffin would be medicine for the soul. Besides, I could ask for directions at the same time.

As I approached the counter a soft-spoken girl in her early twenties said, "Hi. Can I help you?"

I guess I had just come to the very end of my composure because I suddenly burst into tears and began pouring out my heart to her as if she were a $300.00 an hour therapist.

"Yes," I sobbed, "I'm tired, hungry, I've been driving around for an hour trying to find Hobby Lobby and my mother just died . . ."

She interrupted me with wide eyes and gulped, "In the car?"

I instantly stopped crying and stared at her in amazement. "No of course not, she died yesterday!" I said in horror. "What kind of a daughter do you think I am that I would leave my dead mother in the car while I drop by Starbucks for a quick cup of coffee?"

Apparently she didn't know what to say because she just
started laughing. The good news is, so did I. She apologized
saying, "I am so sorry. I just assumed the worst."

How often do we do that? We assume the worst and
have someone convicted of horrible things way before we
know the facts. We need to assume the best. I have gotten
to where I don't believe anything unless I hear it first hand,
and then I still wonder. I also have to remind myself that I
am only hearing one perspective of the story. I am trying to
learn to give people a break. After all, wouldn't I want the
same for myself?

> ## We assume the worst and
> ## have someone convicted of horrible things
> ## way before we know the facts

Secondly, if you are not part of the problem or part of
the solution, stay out of it. I have learned that I have plenty
to juggle without taking on things that are really not mine
to handle. It is easy to stand back and make a judgment
about something you are really no part of. You absolutely
must draw boundaries to protect yourself from being
sucked into the tornado of conflict.

Someone approached me a few years ago complaining
about another friend of mine. "She did this and she did
that ... yak, yak, yak," she said, oozing with anger.

I literally held up my hand and stopped her. "Listen and
listen carefully," I said. "I have no intention of taking sides
and 'setting up camp' on this issue. Common sense tells me

that if I am not part of the problem or part of the solution, then I should stay out of the way. You are both my friends and I refuse to get into the middle of this. It is up to you two to solve the matter."

Unbelievably, she pressed on. I simply looked at her and said, "I mean it," and walked away.

She may have been miffed at me for a while, but it was worth it to not involve myself in a no-win situation that I had no business being a part of.

And the last thing that I try to do upon hearing unnerving information is, as Paul Harvey says, "Find out the rest of the story." Again, we make assumptions and judgments on a tiny fraction of information. There is usually so much more than meets the eye as we saw in the story of the businessman on the subway. You have heard it said, "Everyone has a story", and they do. We need to slow down, not be quick to judge and look beyond the surface.

> **There is usually so much more than meets the eye . . .**

But even after we learn the full story, who are we to make judgment? The clearest example of why it is not our place to judge is given in the New Testament of the Bible. A woman was caught in adultery and the leaders of the community brought her to Jesus to see what his thoughts were on what should be done with her. The leaders said to

Jesus, "She has been found in adultery and by law she is to be stoned to death."

Now by this time a crowd had gathered and already had rocks in their hands ready to fire away. (My question has always been: Where was the guy she was caught with?). Jesus simply answered the crowd, "He who is without sin cast the first stone."

One by one the onlookers dropped the stones they had gathered and walked away.

We always need to take a self-assessment when we're tempted to make hasty assumptions or judgments of others

What a powerful illustration! All of us mess up. Some of our mistakes are just more visible than others. None of us is sinless. We always need to take a self-assessment when we're tempted to make hasty assumptions or judgments of others.

I have a friend who always brings a gift when she comes to visit. Not long after she arrived at my house one time she said, "I brought you something." "Oh?" I said, trying to act surprised, knowing for sure that she had a gift.

I was a little puzzled when she handed me a plain rock with the word "FIRST" written on it. "Thanks Shel," I said, "but what is it and what is it for?"

Slowly she began to recount the trying past year of her life. It had been a doozie! I would have probably gone to bed and pulled the covers over my head and stayed there if

I had been her. She, however, had persevered through the pain and had come out on the other side. She continued, "Suzette, I have learned an incredibly valuable thing through all the junk."

Her ability to find the positive in the middle of the pain is one of the reasons I love and respect her so much. She continued, "Remember the story in the Bible when the woman was caught in adultery and Jesus told the crowd, "He who is without sin cast the first stone?"

I smiled.

"Well, this is your 'first' stone. Never get rid of it. I realize that I cannot even begin to judge the people who have been so unbelievably mean and judgmental of me. It is not my job. Besides, I am not without bad mistakes myself," she finished.

> ## We are human and
> ## as sure as the sun comes up
> ## we will mess up on a daily basis

I have kept that rock by my kitchen sink for years. It is probably one of the most meaningful gifts I have ever received. That simple object asks the question every day, "Who do you think you are Miss Smarty Pants?" It is very humbling and beckons to keep me in balance.

We are all the same. We are human and as sure as the sun comes up we will mess up on a daily basis. I have learned one thing for certain in my life: if I put myself upon a self-built pedestal, I will fall off and land flat on my fanny every time. No one died and put me on the throne of judgment. It is not my job and one I really don't want. My job is to love, encourage, extend grace and pray that others do the same for me.

Something to think about...

▶ Is there a person in your life you possibly may have misjudged?

Note

1. Story originally told in Steven Covey's book, *Daily Reflections for Highly Effective People: Living the "7 Habits of Highly Effective People" Every Day* (Simon & Schuster, 1989).

Church Ain't Over
'til the Fat Lady Sings

"Our greatest weakness lies in giving up.
The most certain way to succeed
is to try one more time."
(Thomas Edison)

There wasn't a long list of rules at the Brawner house when we were growing up, but the ones we had were pretty concrete. Taking drivers ed, keyboarding and study hall in high school was basically non-negotiable. We didn't have set curfews, but if we were going to be later than the agreed upon time, calling home was a must. According to Dad, disrespecting Mom almost put you on America's Most Wanted list. A major hard and fast rule was, you finish what you start. The primary purpose, I'm sure, was to teach us to follow through with commitments. However, with three kids who wanted to try out everything, the rule also was most likely for our parents' sanity.

"Just do it" turned into "just keep on doing it"

Time was measured by the school calendar. If we started a sport or extra curricular activity we stayed with it until the end of the season or school year. My freshman year of high school I remember wishing I had thought through basketball more carefully before the season began. I had played in grade school and junior high so it only seemed right to continue in high school. Besides my best friends were playing, and that was really more important to me than basketball itself. The trips, summer camps, and after game get-togethers were why I laced up my shoes. Then things took an unexpected turn when Coach moved me because the center on the varsity team injured her ankle. That meant I had to leave my friends, so my motivation to even be on the basketball court was instantly gone. The next four months dragged slowly by. I knew I had to hang in and finish the season. "Just do it" turned into "just keep on doing it". A huge relief along with a slight sense of accomplishment came at the sound of the final buzzer of the last game. I had made it through! That was the end of my basketball career and the beginning of my understanding of "Church Ain't Over 'til the Fat Lady Sings".

Perseverance and commitment are tough whether it is to a cause, a job, a person, or a family, because they involve one thing – a lot of work. When something is fresh and new it's fun and challenging. Just like a car, though, the new smell eventually wears off and then what? Things may begin to reek like a three-week-old banana in the glove box. That is when we need to buckle in, put it in four-wheel drive, hang on and keep on going. It's easy when we are cruising along on a traffic-free smooth interstate. But when all of a sudden we hit construction and detours we begin to second-guess our decisions. Many times if we press on through the detour we end back up on the smooth interstate again.

> **Perseverance and commitment are tough whether it is to a cause, a job, a person, or a family because they involve one thing – a lot of work**

Giving up has been made so acceptable. Everything seems so "drive-through" and disposable these days. If we find that something is more of a challenge than we bargained for, we back out. If we don't like something, we throw it away and get a new or better one. Instant gratification feels so much better than delayed. We want everything two days ago. We are envious of those around us who seem to have it all together. However, we don't stop for one minute to consider all of the day-in and day-out long hours that have been part of the process. The good stuff involves working hard and sometimes waiting for what seems forever, but our vision gets blurred and the long haul seems hardly worth it.

For most of us the long haul is a detour or a season in life. For some, though, the long haul is life itself. In Arkansas in 1953 a baby boy was born with cerebral palsy. After struggling through the first years of his life, tragically at fourteen he was orphaned then bounced from family to family with nowhere to really call home. He withstood ridicule and constant discouragement but even in the face of seemingly unbeatable odds, the words *give up* never drifted into his vocabulary.

> **The good stuff involves working hard**
> **and sometimes waiting for**
> **what seems forever,**
> **but our vision gets blurred and**
> **the long haul seems hardly worth it**

Though the first part of his life looked like he wouldn't make it, David Ring never bought into that theory. Teaming bulldog determination with a clear understanding of God's purpose for his life, he pushed forward as if he were handicap free. He and his wife, Karen, have four children. Every year he speaks to thousands in churches, corporate groups and conventions sharing his message of motivation and hope. David is extremely witty and steeped in insight. Even though most mornings simply getting out of bed is a painful and difficult task, he never asks why? He only asks, why not? As he begins each event, he very bluntly says in his slurred speech, "I have Cerebral Palsy. What is your problem?"

We all have problems and giving up too soon may be one of them. How many marriages today simply fail because we aren't willing to take the time to look at wounds and figure out how to turn them into wisdom? Love at first sight is amazing, but love after fifty years is even more amazing. How many people leave one job because they don't like the boss simply to find a tougher boss at the next job? I haven't been there yet, but evidently the hang-in-there theory is one to also latch onto when parenting. Our friend, Karen, was at a luncheon where several moms were discussing the trials of raising teenagers. She sat quietly and listened as each mother complained. One of the women finally turned to Karen and said, "You are so lucky. Your daughter is such a good kid!"

> **Love at first sight is amazing, but love after fifty years is even more amazing**

She calmly responded, "I don't think luck had anything to do with it. It has taken eighteen years of hard work and commitment."

Anything worth having or worth doing is worth the effort. The kicker is that a lot of sweat equity is usually involved.

Commitment is something that takes up time and uses up a lot of energy. It's no wonder that we tend give up so easily. However, before we pick up some heavy guilt baggage, let's realize that there is a difference between giving up and making a change. We've all been in situations where we're suddenly jarred with the realization that change would be a good thing.

Hebrews 12:1 encourages us to, *"throw off everything that hinders and the sin that so easily entangles, and let us run with perseverance the race marked out for us."* NASCAR is the largest, most popular spectator sport in the United States. The drivers of those finely tuned, amazingly fast cars are focused on one thing: crossing the finish line. During the course of the race they may run into obstacles and have mechanical problems. Occasionally they have to pull off into the pit to refuel and have the tires changed. They want to make the adjustments and get right back on the track as quickly as possible. During the race they have to make the necessary corrections in their strategy to run the best race that they can.

So it should be with us. We are all in a race of some kind. At times we need to make adjustments then hop back into the race.

Anne graduated from high school with honors and went through college on a full scholarship. Her dad, mom and brother all were college professors, so it only seemed right that she follow them. After her undergraduate work, she was awarded a graduate assistant job while she was working on her Masters degree. But Anne was miserable. She finally gathered up the courage to tell her family that she was so sorry, but not one thread of her fiber wanted to teach. What she really wanted to do was be a dentist. She had to make a change and go after what she wanted to do with her life. And she did, without ever looking back.

"When the horse is dead, it's time to dismount"

Many times in our life we might find ourselves at a crossroads where choices need to be made. There is wisdom in the old Native American saying, "When the horse is dead, it's time to dismount." Anne was riding a "dead horse". Her heart was not in what she was doing. She was simply trying to keep peace in her family by living the dream they had for her, not the one she had for herself. She needed to make the change, go after her dream, and not feel like she was a quitter. She was finally breaking loose and going after what she had given up in the first place. We should evaluate what we are doing with our lives and consider if it's what we want or if it's what someone else wants for us. Basically, the challenge is searching our heart and finding the balance somewhere between *staying strong* and *staying stuck*.

Stopping on third base adds no more to the score than striking out. That says something to me. Why quit if you have come this far? I was discouraged once, wanting to stop dead in my tracks and give up on something I really wanted, and a friend said to me, "God didn't bring you this far to drop you off. Keep on going."

Stopping on third base
adds no more to the score
than striking out

Persistence and commitment are a decision. We make the choice to bail out or stay in during the tough stuff. We always come out better and stronger on the other side for having gone through the gunk. Besides, how you start is not nearly as important as how you finish.

Persistence and commitment
are a decision

I watched a man while I was growing up who I know is deeply committed. He doesn't know my name and I don't know his, but I saw him just about every day. And he smiled. Today he still takes a walk through town barely shuffling along with his cane. It's that kind of a shuffle that gets you to the bathroom in the middle of the night when you are still mostly asleep. Determined and with a purpose. He must be extremely committed to that walk every day because no matter what the weather, he shuffles down the sidewalk one foot in front of the other. He is not an old man, but it is evident that he has had a stroke or an accident of some kind that has crippled him. I so admire his tenacity and commitment to keep on moving. How easy it would be for him to just sit down, but he keeps on going! I think of my no-name friend when I am tired and consider: if he can shuffle, I can keep on going. That type of commitment should be coveted. Commitment to put one foot in front of the other ... no matter what.

Who is the fat lady anyway? Just as familiar as the portly woman in a Viking costume and blonde pigtails belting out the end of an opera, was the lady singing "Just As I Am" to signal the end of a rural Sunday church service in the south years ago. My grandmother said that summer Sundays would get so hot and uncomfortable that sometimes she would almost stick to the hard wooden pew. However, as soon as the big woman with too much rouge in a flowered dress stepped up to sing, the kids knew the covered-dish lunch was about ready to begin. It was like a blast of cool air seeing her approach the platform and it made the wait worthwhile. But before she sang, church was in session and perseverance to sit still and hang on was just necessary.

Life is complicated and often downright hard. It gets uncomfortable like that hot church pew a lot of times, but we need to remember to hang on and push on through. Yogi Berra, the great baseball legend, said, "It's not over until it's over." Until the last out is made, there is always a chance to win.

Every once in a while when I am completely worn out, I think I hear the lady tuning up. Then I stop and consider everything and realize that it is definitely not over yet. I guess I will finally let her sing in that big flowered dress at my funeral.

Something to think about...

▶ When are you most tempted to give up?

Afterthoughts

Like a trip back in time, visitors to our community can take a horse and carriage ride through old downtown and along the lakeshore. It's almost calming to listen to the clog, clog, clog of the horse's hooves on the pavement unless you are in a hurry and get stuck behind one. This past July I drove by the spot where buggies normally sit only to see a sign that read: CLOSED FROM NOON UNTIL 6PM, TOO HOT! I smiled and thought how nice it would be if we all could just close up shop when things get too uncomfortable. Many of us might end up staying in the shut down mode the majority of the time because there is one thing for sure: life is tough.

There is so much we don't have control over. We can, however, control how we treat others, how we act and how we react to life. It simply boils down to the choices we make. If only we could remember the power of our words, the pricelessness of not being judgmental, and that we all should allow some "Do-Overs". If we could regain a sense of commitment and most importantly lighten up and laugh a lot even when all we really want to do is cry, things might begin to level out.

When we get lost in the maze of everyday living, we forget to slow down and enjoy the moment. The distractions of a past that haunts us or worries about a future we can do absolutely nothing about, tend to cloud our vision. When we put our life on pause and let the "now" come into focus, the fog that keeps us from enjoying the present might slowly lift. The secret hides in the slowing down. Sometimes it is easier to keep moving at a frantic pace because if we slow down too long and get intimate with our thoughts it can be frightening.

Probably one of the scariest things a parent does is watch a child pull away from home on his or her first solo trip driving a car. It might only be a two-mile trek to the grocery store, but it is a gigantic milestone. Having been the child and the parent I am really not sure who is more anxious; the one with sweaty palms behind the wheel or the one with sweaty palms staring out the window wondering how on earth that baby could be old enough to drive.

My Dad thought he should be the one to teach me to drive. I still wonder why Mom agreed to turn us loose since she always questioned Dad's driving ability. We laughed a lot and had a few close calls, but I was ready when I finally pulled out of the driveway by myself.

We always turned onto Pine Manor Drive after we left the house. It was a narrow road lined with very tall pine trees and very deep ditches. I would hold my breath as if I were under water when I drove down that road, praying there would be no oncoming cars. One time Dad noticed how tightly I was gripping the steering wheel and asked,

"Suzette, why are you so nervous? You are doing a great job."

"The road is so narrow and the ditches are so deep. I will be in a real mess if I make one mistake," I answered, keeping both eyes focused straight ahead.

He laughed and said something that made that scary drive seem so simple. "If you really think about it, all you have to do is keep it between the ditches."

Isn't that the way it is with life? Things get so complicated in this hamster wheel of a world we live in. We are faced with so many choices, decisions and cross-roads that every day can seem like a Pine Manor Drive with tall pines and deep ditches. What we really want and need is balance. That special place lies somewhere between too much and not enough. And just where is that? Some-where between the ditches.

A little bit of common sense, the comfort of God's guidance and the understanding of His unconditional love, even when we get off into the ditch, somehow makes the trip not only bearable, but very exciting. Blessings to you while you "keep it between the ditches" on your life's journey.

About the Authors

Suzette Brawner

Being a motivational speaker, an award winning author, a wife of thirty-five years, the mother of three married kids and her newest role as grandmother, keeps Suzette Brawner on the cutting edge of *real life*. Nothing staged, nothing fabricated, just honest-to-goodness real life. She and her husband, Jim, live outside Branson, Missouri.

Jill Brawner Jones

An actress trained in New York and Los Angeles, Jill is a member of the Screen Actors Guild (SAG) and the American Federation of Television and Radio Artists (AFTRA). She is passionate about encouraging women to enjoy life to the fullest. Jill and her husband, David, live in Los Angeles, California.

To contact the authors for speaking engagements e-mail Jim@teambarnabas.com

We hope you enjoyed reading this New Wine book.
For details of other New Wine books
and a range of 2,000 titles from other
Word and Spirit publishers visit our website:
www.newwineministries.co.uk